Lull Before Dark

Lull before dark

Caroline Gourlay

BROOKS BOOKS
Decatur, Illinois

Lull Before Dark
ISBN: 1-929820-09-7

Copyright @ 2005 by Caroline Gourlay
Printed in the United States of America

First Edition

Brooks Books
3720 N. Woodridge Drive
Decatur, Illinois 62526 USA

http://www.brooksbookshaiku.com
brooksbooks@sbcglobal.net

to my Mother
1913-1989

PREFACE FROM THE EDITORS

With each successive reading of *Lull Before Dark*, we hope the reader becomes more engrossed with Caroline Gourlay's haiku. Full of earthly creatures, heartfelt moments, light, dark, and everything in between, this collection not only brings us closer to the Welsh countryside—which often serves as her inspiration—but also brings us closer to the root of humanity, to the simple moments that give our lives meaning.

Attention has been given to the movement of the collection, the flow that lets the reader drift as they read without any sudden jumps or halting interruptions. Editor and author exchanged multiple versions of this collection in order to achieve an order and format that best suits the chapbook. Like the hidden bird in the following haiku, the end result can seem distant in the beginning, with only small glimpses of the eventual whole.

> hidden blue tit
> his song advancing
> branch by branch

The editors of Brooks Books invite you to enter into the *Lull Before Dark* by Caroline Gourlay. Take your time and lose yourself in the seen and the unseen, the sunsets and the winds, the earth and the sky of these beautiful, evocative haiku.

Randy Brooks, Editor
Katherine B. Steimann, Student Editor

A READER'S INTRODUCTION

Haiku is the power of a few carefully chosen words to propel us into a heightened perception and understanding of the world we live in. Haiku inspires you to embrace the images presented and make them your own, appreciating the gift the author has given you. Haiku may be defined as a simple, brief poem containing a seasonal reference and employing a crafty method of "cutting," but anyone who truly knows and loves haiku will tell you that defining the techniques of writing will never do justice to the essence of haiku. H.F. Noyes once said, "What is most vital is that we expose ourselves to the *spirit* of the art form" (*The Loose Thread* 135).

With this spirit in mind, I encourage you to delve into the works of Caroline Gourlay, a celebrated English haiku poet and editor. Ms. Gourlay has written poetry for many years, and she became an active member of the haiku community in 1994. She spent three years as editor of *Blithe Spirit*, and has published several collections. Gourlay's haiku instantly attracted me because of the range of experiences her work deals with and also the simple, beautiful language she employs.

What strikes me as most fascinating about Gourlay's haiku is her ability to both play by the "rules" and experiment at the same time. Many times, while reading examples of her haiku, I found pieces that did not seem to have clear images; in fact, many of them seemed to be built around an abstraction. While this generally runs contrary to what is deemed necessary for a "good haiku," I believe that Gourlay has not crossed the boundary into meaningless sentiment.

In her essay entitled, "Some Thoughts on the Writing of Haiku and Other Poems," published in *The Loose Thread* (2001), Gourlay writes: "Every good haiku points to the here and now, whether it deals with a moment relating to nature or human nature, or successfully links the two—moments of intense awareness that can only be arrived at during those comparatively rare moments when we are truly living in the present" (123). It is these moments when the writer of the haiku must make decisions—conscious decisions—of what memories to keep and what memories to destroy.

One cannot approach this type of poetry with a purely analytical eye. Analysis and critique have their place, certainly, but a reader must also surrender themselves to the beauty and simplicity that is haiku. Reading and appreciating Caroline Gourlay's fine haiku has increased my love for this literary art form, not only the technique and elements of writing, but also the power encompassed in these simple lines. "A good haiku must demonstrate the only reality, which is the present," says Gourlay, "and will come out of an awareness of the true nature of existence" (*The Loose Thread* 122). Gourlay's haiku point us to that truth; her haiku are her eyes to the world, and we should thank her for the opportunity to see her reality.

Maureen Ritter
Global Haiku Traditions Student
Millikin University, Spring 2004

log fire—
turning in the flames
my watched thoughts

touching you
as you lie sleeping—
the days shorten

winter evening—
after the train has left,
the snowbound road

sinking sun
taking the mountain
with it

frosty morning—
the skitter of calves hooves
on concrete

bent with age
he cuts from the hedge
the straightest stick

winter chill—
catching the look
in your eye

ahead in line—
his laughter from behind
catching me up

radio play—
listening for your footsteps
on the stairs

afterwards
the pulse in your throat
faster

school bus gone...
the snowman's smile widens
into the afternoon

slipping
through melting snow
the barn roof

into the restaurant
ten paces behind her
new blouse

touching it—
early spring sunshine
on this wet stone

all those things
I wish now I'd asked you—
snow falling

first March warmth
poised above its claws
the buzzard

white water
bursting from the hillside
thorn blossom

not wanting to talk ...
my shadow detaches
from the group

water reflections
flowing up the trunk
of the bowed alder

spring torrents...
a cascade of bluebells
through the wood

early morning mist
gathering in the lane
cow-parsley

my mother—
after her death
her silence

clap of thunder
shaking the meadow grass
a mayfly

talking talking—
the shower continues
under the trees

as if
it had never heard of spring
this house in the wood

napping on the bank—
a small stream trickles
through the afternoon

newborn baby
fragile as eggshell
the blue sky

Letters Home...
on the dedication page
your handwriting

hidden blue tit
his song advancing
branch by branch

chief executive
loosening his tie
sniffs a dog-rose

following it
out of the village—
spring sunshine

your tirade—
steam rises from the
coffee cup

the pass narrows
a dung beetle on his way
blocks our path

in drenching rain
two young girls without coats
eat wild raspberries

his tattooed arms—
hotter on my shoulders
the midday sun

below the door
of the photo booth
unlaced shoes

out-stared by the child
I drop my eyes to my book
and pretend to read...

last few miles—
clouds carried by
the river

leaving the hills
in my rear view mirror
last day of summer

storm buffets the house
my hand starts to massage
the cat's shoulder

the rain stops
and the silent house fills
with empty rooms

again no word...
on the map only inches
to your island shore

long walk home
between one step and the next
letting it drop

crossing
the woodland floor
a fly

talk of war—
the noonday sun sharpens
a holly leaf

wanting to see
round the next corner
I turn the page

sunset flares
lighting up the windows
of the empty house

unseen voices
rustling the curtains
summer wind

alone in the house
my unvoiced diatribe
scores a bulls-eye

I close my book—
a wave breaks its silence
against the rocks

photo chance...
again I capture
only your smile

wind getting up—
stirring the dark water
unwanted feelings

ugh! a rat...
but your eyes meet mine
as you die

harvest finished—
the empty field fills
with moonlight

watching a stoat
I become the landscape
he moves towards

staying on—
late summer stretches across
the empty yard

tired-looking doctor
holding my urine sample
talks about Schubert

apology—
a burst of green sun
through the dock leaf

turning for home
in the lull before dark
blackberries

sound of footsteps—
hidden in the long grass
fallen apples

writing to you—
the tardy autumn sun
falls short of the hill

grassed-over path
the junction of not knowing
which way to turn

your voice falters...
the blue rolling hills fade
into the distance

last day packing
in the empty fruit bowl
a fly settles

dawn departure...
leaving the flowers behind
on the table

the red rambler
you last saw in bud
drops a petal

September sun
last seen on the curve
of this rosehip

first autumn winds—
a finger post points down
the empty path

awake all night—
a gale bends the poplar trees
to breaking point

high tide
against the sea wall
night breaking

lonely beach—
surfing the Scots Pines
dawn wind

rippling across
the empty swimming pool
leaf shadows

unopened letter—
a kestrel hovers
in the distance

rendezvous...
running out of daylight
autumn evening

not looking back—
remembering the light
on an oak apple

letting it ring...
I watch the sun leave
the mountain top

falling asleep...
the sound of water
growing darker

October frost—
under the deckchair
green grass

in your hand, leaves—
all the reds of the season
punched and bruised

late for it...
I lead my shadow
by the foot

fogbound road—
walking on the inside
of the inside world

eating in silence...
the elongated fingers
of the icon

Angelus...
from deep in the wood
an owl calls

a child's outstretched hand—
both eyes of the Buddha
closed

zazen-sitting
watching through closed eyes
the rising sun

walking meditation—
the motionless branches
of the spindle tree

days getting colder
a fallen branch
lies across the path

old diary—
this beech leaf still green
between the pages

New Year's eve
overtaken by clouds
the young moon

early morning
sliding over the ridge
a path of sun

falling snow...
the branches of the oak tree
take shape

winter dusk—
in the blue of my mind
the skylark's song

path running out...
a rabbit's footprints
fill with snow

across snowy fields
the white undersides
of the running deer

just
for this moment
that cloud

frozen ground—
then the sun melts your voice
into my bloodstream

evening firelight
drawing the dark corners
into the room

last light
holding the water
holding the trees

SENRYU

The following senryu are included in this collection:

ABOUT THE AUTHOR

Caroline Gourlay lives with her husband on the Welsh Border and has written poetry for much of her life. She became involved with the haiku movement in 1994, joining the British Haiku Society that year and the Haiku Society of America somewhat later. She edited *Blithe Spirit* for three years from 1998-2000 and is a Patron of the Ledbury Poetry Festival in England.

Her publications include *Crossing The Field* (Redlake Press, 1995), *Through The Cafe Door* (Snapshot Press, 2000), *Reading All Night* (Hub Press, 1999), *Against the Odds* (Hub Press, 2001) and *This Country* (Poetry Monthly Press, 2005).

Her haiku and tanka have appeared in several journals and anthologies. She had five tanka among the winners of the 1997 Tanka Splendor Award and won the James Hackett Award for haiku in 1996.

ACKNOWLEDGMENTS

Special thanks to the editors and publishers of the following magazines, where
many of these haiku originally appeared in print:

> *Blithe Spirit, British Haiku Society Anthology "Flat",*
> *British Haiku Society Anthology "Hidden", Frogpond,*
> *Haiku Spirit, Modern Haiku, Noon, Presence,*
> *Simply Haiku, Snapshots Calendar 2005*

Cover photo by Alida Duff, graphic design student, Millikin University.

Additional photos by Laura Podeschi, graphic design student, Millikin University.

Reader's introduction by Maureen Ritter, an English education student, Millikin University.

Special thanks to Katherine Steimann, student editor from Millikin University, who helped
review, arrange and design this chapbook as part of an internship with Brooks Books in the
Spring of 2005.